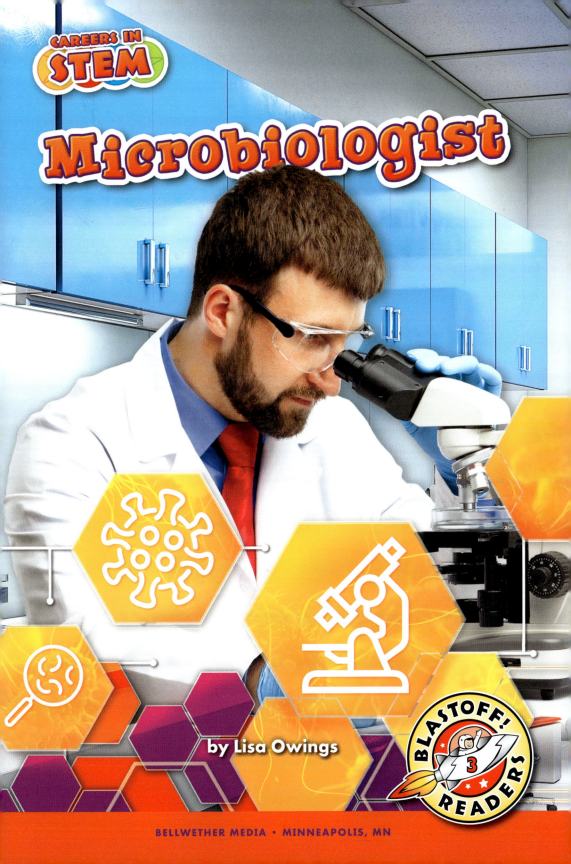

Blastoff! Readers are carefully developed by literacy experts to build reading stamina and move students toward fluency by combining standards-based content with developmentally appropriate text.

 Level 1 provides the most support through repetition of high-frequency words, light text, predictable sentence patterns, and strong visual support.

 Level 2 offers early readers a bit more challenge through varied sentences, increased text load, and text-supportive special features.

 Level 3 advances early-fluent readers toward fluency through increased text load, less reliance on photos, advancing concepts, longer sentences, and more complex special features.

★ **Blastoff! Universe**

Reading Level

 Grade K

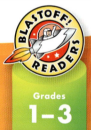 Grades 1–3

 Grade 4

This edition first published in 2024 by Bellwether Media, Inc.

No part of this publication may be reproduced in whole or in part without written permission of the publisher. For information regarding permission, write to Bellwether Media, Inc., Attention: Permissions Department, 6012 Blue Circle Drive, Minnetonka, MN 55343.

Library of Congress Cataloging-in-Publication Data

LC record for Microbiologist available at: https://lccn.loc.gov/2023001657

Text copyright © 2024 by Bellwether Media, Inc. BLASTOFF! READERS and associated logos are trademarks and/or registered trademarks of Bellwether Media, Inc.

Editor: Betsy Rathburn   Designer: Andrea Schneider

Printed in the United States of America, North Mankato, MN.

Table of Contents

Keeping People Healthy	4
What Is a Microbiologist?	6
At Work	10
Becoming a Microbiologist	16
Glossary	22
To Learn More	23
Index	24

Keeping People Healthy

A microbiologist works in a **lab**. He is studying a **virus**.

He will use what he learns to make a new **vaccine**. It will keep people healthy!

vaccine

lab

What Is a Microbiologist?

microscope

microbes

Microbiologists study tiny **microbes**. There are many kinds of microbes. They are found everywhere on Earth!

Microbiologists test microbe **samples** in labs. They use powerful **microscopes** to see them.

Microbiology in Real Life

healthier crops

medicines

cheese

They learn about microbes that cause illness. They use these to make new medicines.

Famous Microbiologist

Name: Peter Piot

Born: February 17, 1949

Birthplace: Leuven, Belgium

Schooling: Ghent University, University of Antwerp

Known For: Led work to control the spread of HIV/AIDS

Some find microbes that help Earth. Others work to make healthier crops!

At Work

Some microbiologists work in health care. They learn what makes people sick.

They track how illness spreads. They make new ways to fight it!

microbes that cause illness

microbes in soil

Some study how microbes affect Earth. They look at soil and water. They remove harmful microbes.

Others work to keep Earth clean. They find helpful microbes. Some help clean oil spills!

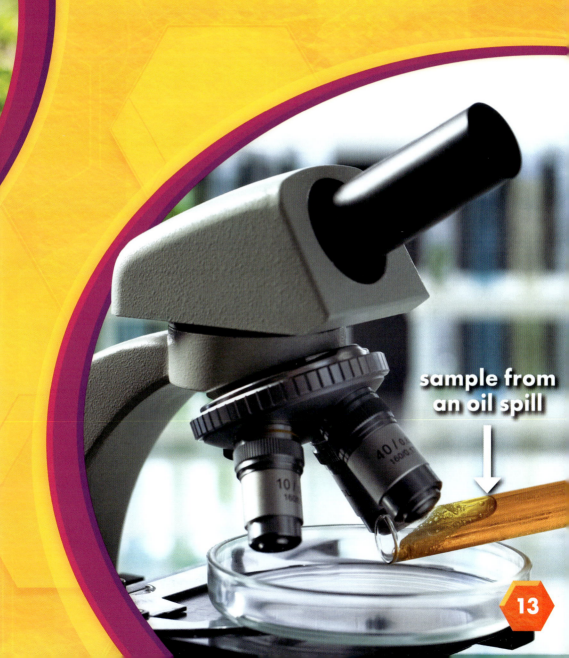

sample from an oil spill

Some use microbes to change plants. They make crops stronger.

Using STEM

Science — study how microbes affect Earth

Technology — use microscopes

Engineering — create stronger crops

Math — count samples

microbes in cheese

Some use microbes in food.
They make cheese or bread.
They make sure it is safe.
They make it taste good!

Becoming a Microbiologist

Microbiologists go to college. They take math classes. They take science classes. They learn to set up lab tests.

Most go to **graduate school**. They choose a subject to focus on.

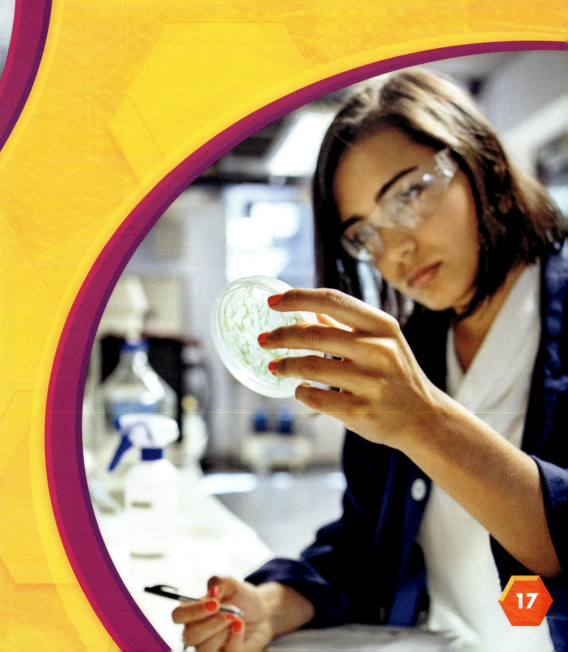

Then they find a job. They work on a team. They help others with **research**.

They gain hands-on skills. They share what they learn.

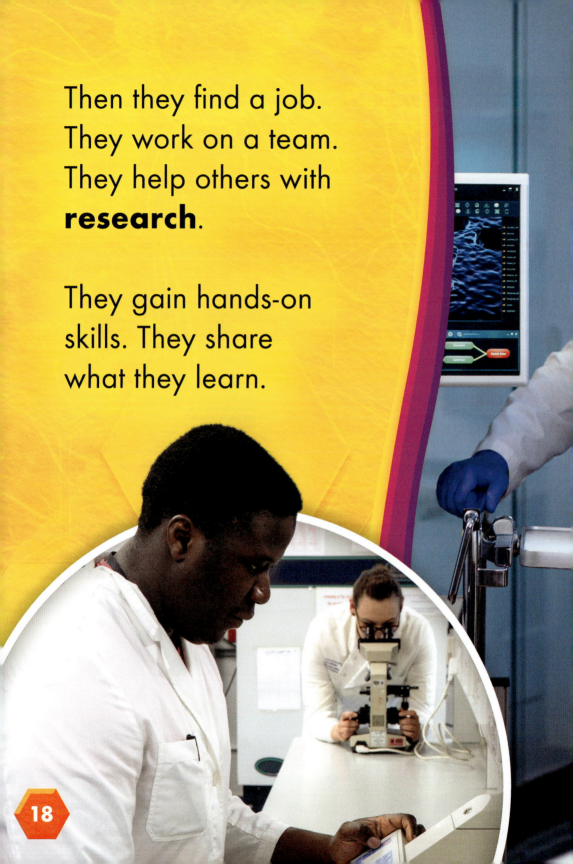

They may lead their own research. Some teach classes. They write and speak well. They pay attention to details.

How to Become a Microbiologist

1. study science in college
2. learn lab skills
3. go to graduate school
4. find a job

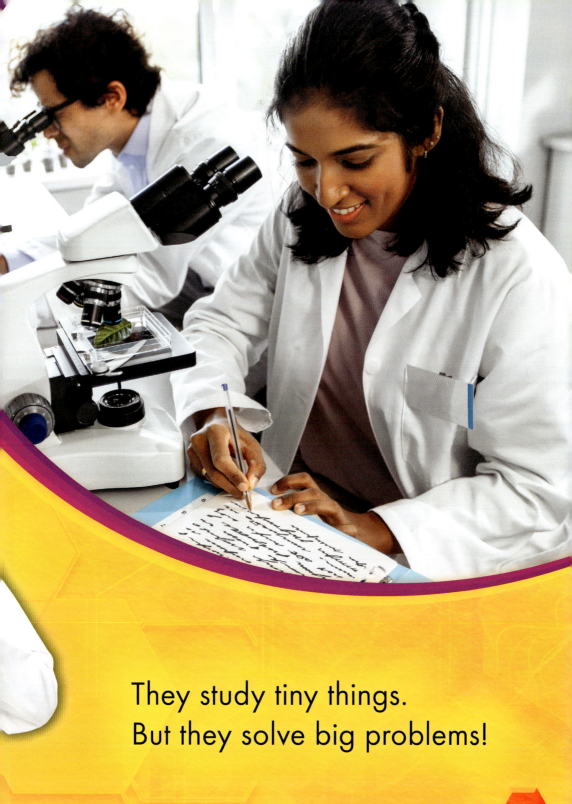

They study tiny things.
But they solve big problems!

Glossary

graduate school—a school where people can study a specialty area after college

lab—a building or room with special tools to do science experiments and tests

microbes—things that can be seen only with a microscope, such as viruses and bacteria

microscopes—tools used for looking at very small things

research—careful study to find new knowledge or information about something

samples—small amounts of things that give information about where they were taken from

vaccine—a medicine created to keep people from getting illnesses

virus—a microbe that causes illnesses in living things

To Learn More

AT THE LIBRARY

Heos, Bridget. *I'm a Virus!* New York, N.Y.: Crown Books for Young Readers, 2022.

Mould, Steve. *The Bacteria Book*. New York, N.Y.: DK/Penguin Random House, 2018.

Rajcak, Hélène, and Damien Laverdunt. *Unseen Worlds: Real-Life Microscopic Creatures Hiding All Around Us*. Tonbridge, U.K.: What on Earth Books, 2019.

ON THE WEB

FACTSURFER

Factsurfer.com gives you a safe, fun way to find more information.

1. Go to www.factsurfer.com.

2. Enter "microbiologist" into the search box and click 🔍.

3. Select your book cover to see a list of related content.

Index

college, 16
crops, 9, 14
food, 15
graduate school, 17
health care, 10
how to become, 20
illness, 8, 10
job, 18
lab, 4, 5, 7, 16
math, 16
medicines, 8
microbes, 6, 7, 8, 9, 10, 12, 13, 14, 15
microbiology in real life, 7
microscopes, 6, 7

oil spills, 13
Piot, Peter, 8
research, 18, 20
samples, 7
science, 16
soil, 12
team, 18
using STEM, 14
vaccine, 4
virus, 4
water, 12

The images in this book are reproduced through the courtesy of: Billion Pictures, front cover (microbiologist); urfin, front cover (background); grebcha, p. 3; LookerStudio, p. 4; DC Studio, pp. 4-5 (lab), 18-19; YAKOBCHUK VIACHESLAV, pp. 6-7 (microscope); Wikipedia, p. 6 (microbes); Krasula, p. 7 (healthier crops); i viewfinder, p. 7 (medicines); Natalia Van Donick, p. 7 (cheese); Anwar Hussein/Alamy, p. 8 (Peter Piot); alexander raths, pp. 8-9; AnaLysiStudiO, p. 10; aslysun, pp. 10-11; kaninstudio, pp. 12-13; Rattiya Thongdumhyu, p. 12 (microbes in soil); Motortion, p. 13; gefotostock/ Alamy, pp. 14-15; kateryna kon, p. 15 (microbes in cheese); Morsa Images/ Getty Images, pp. 16-17; NickyLloyd, p. 17; Peter Devlin/ Alamy, p. 18; Innovatedcaptures, p. 20 (microbiologist); Ground Picture, pp. 20-21; Hong Vo, pp. 22-23 (cheese).